THIS BOOK BELONGS TO

oooooooooooooooooooooooooooooooooooo

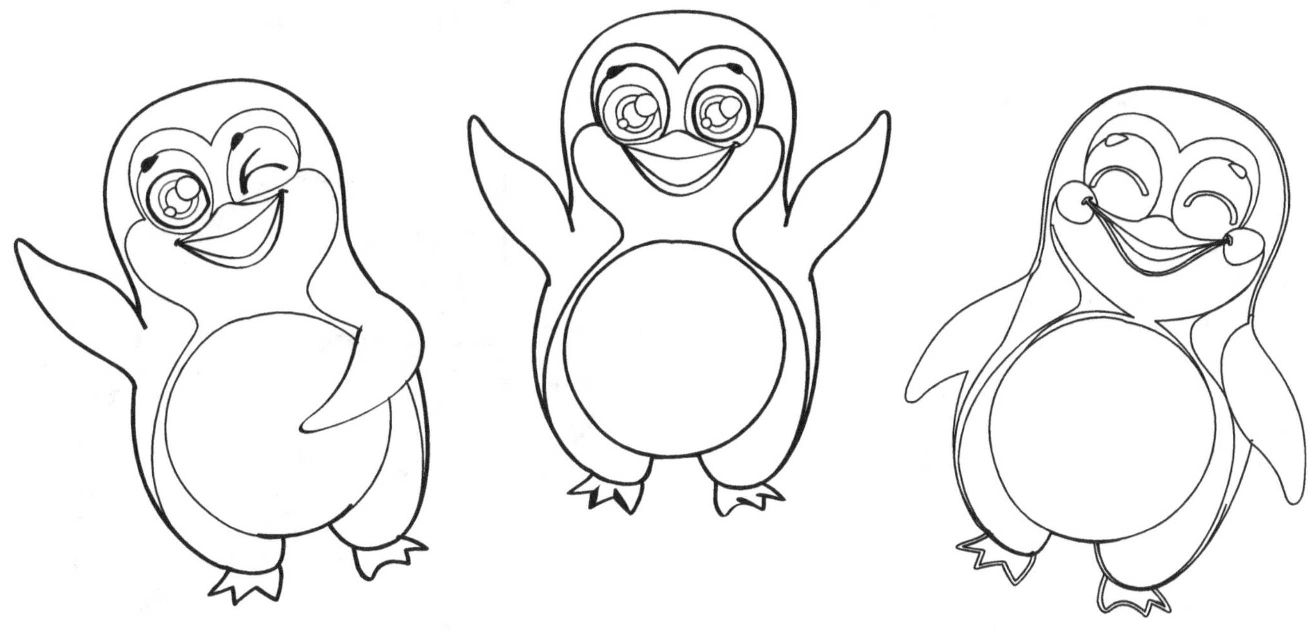

1

COLOR TEST

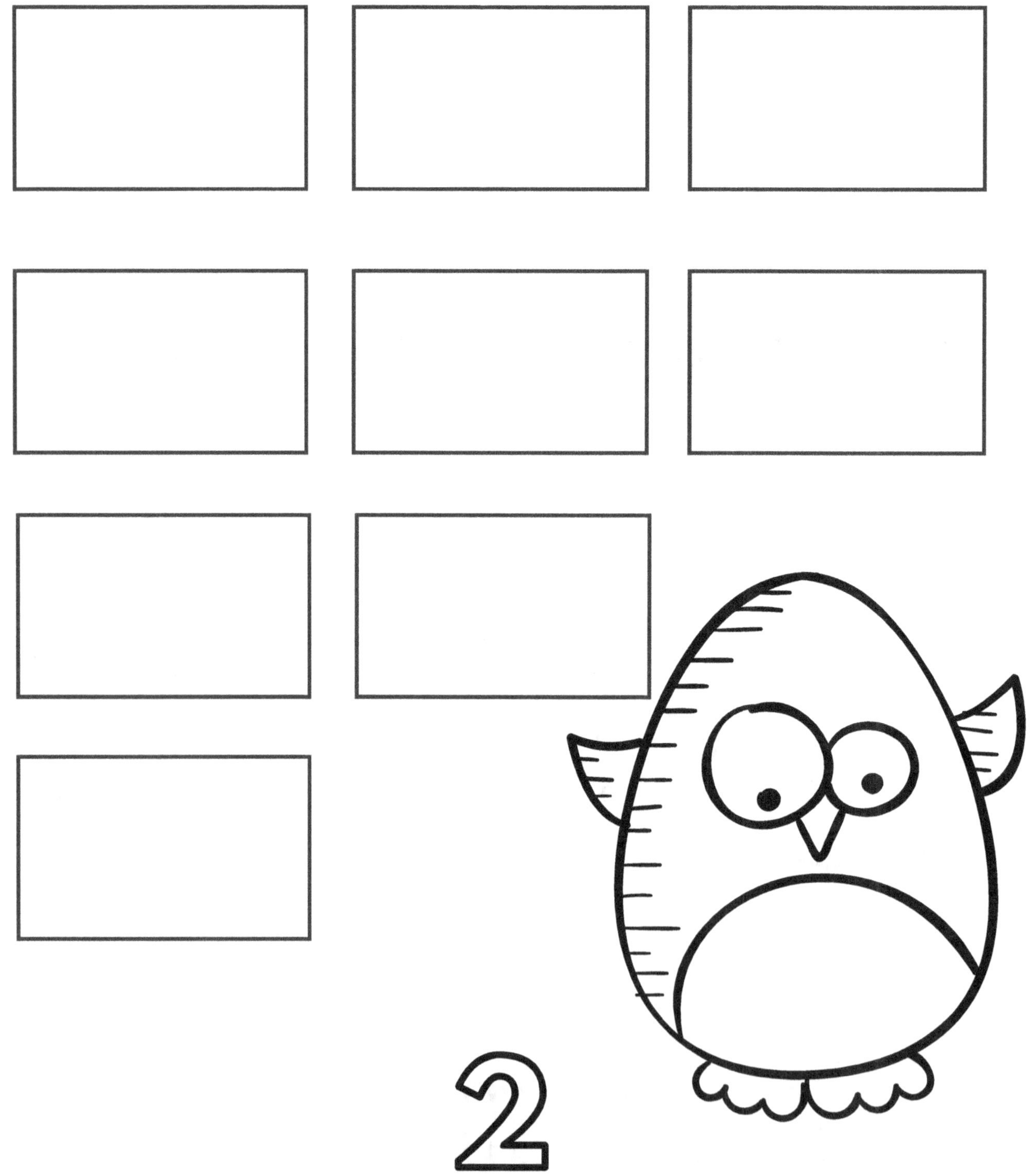

REPEAT

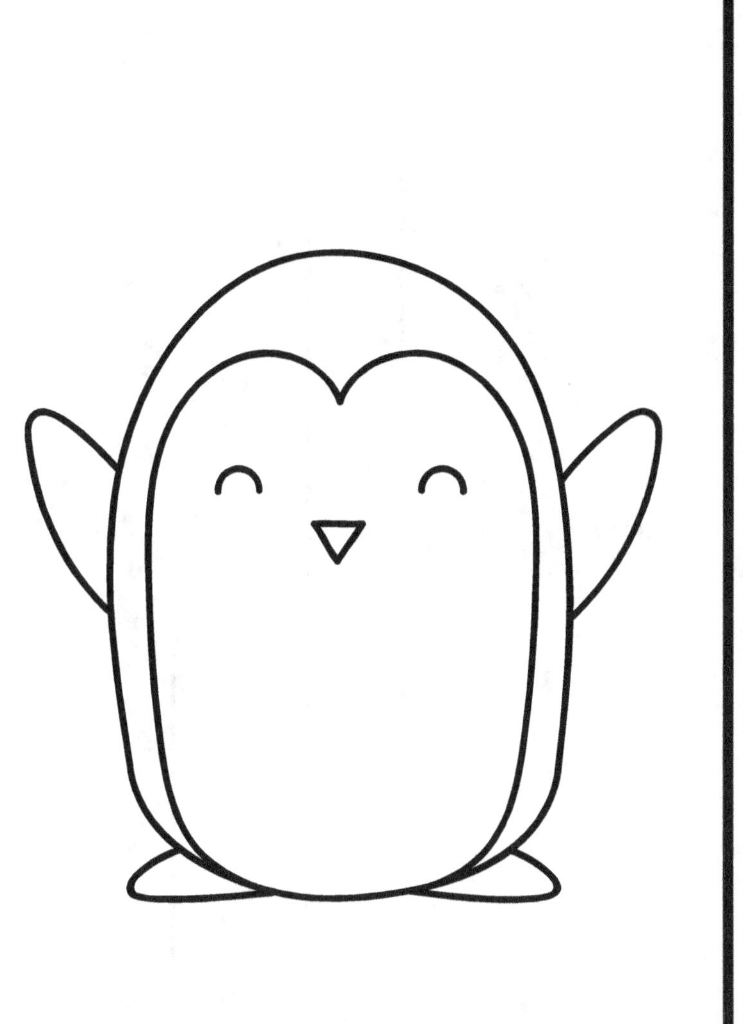

3

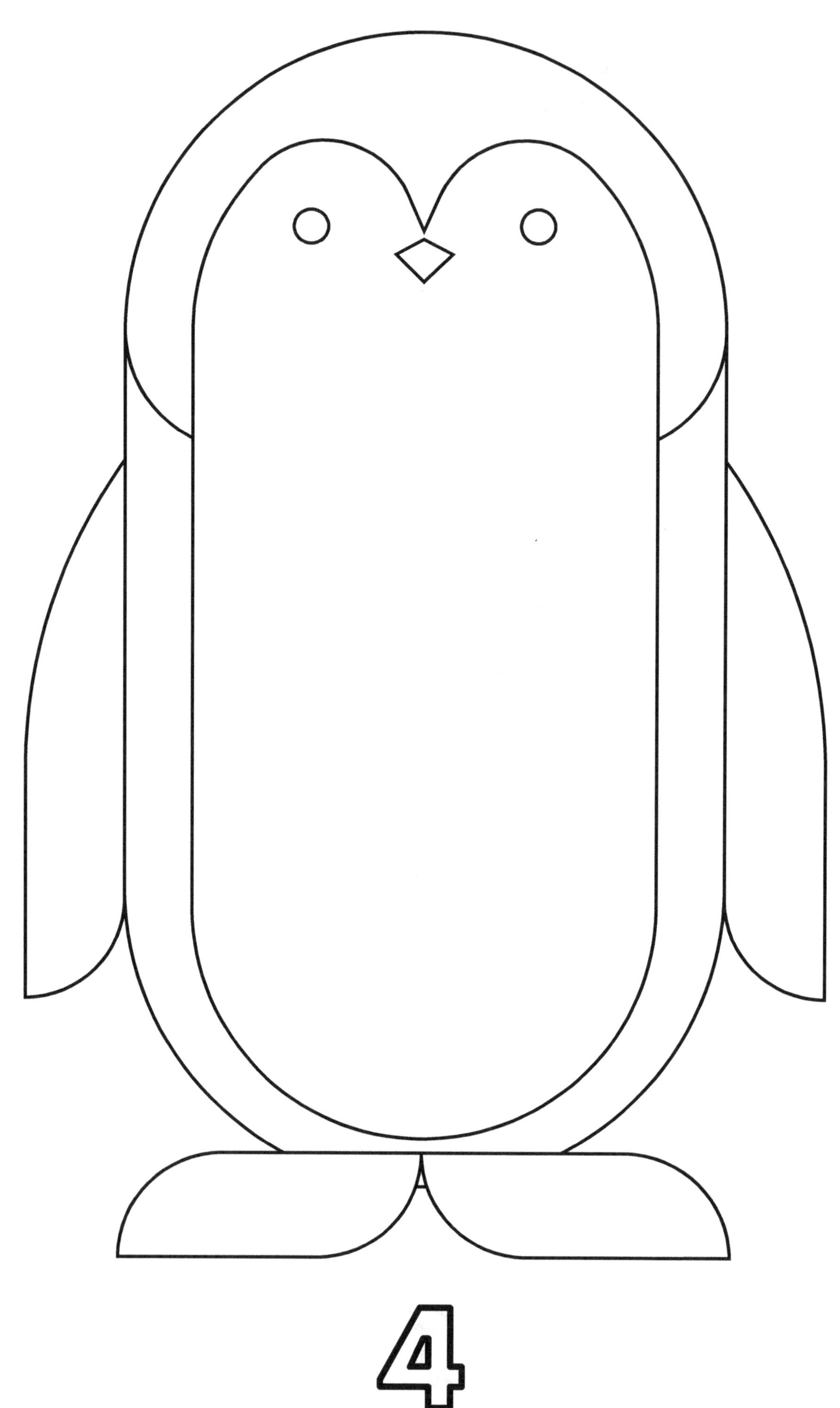

4

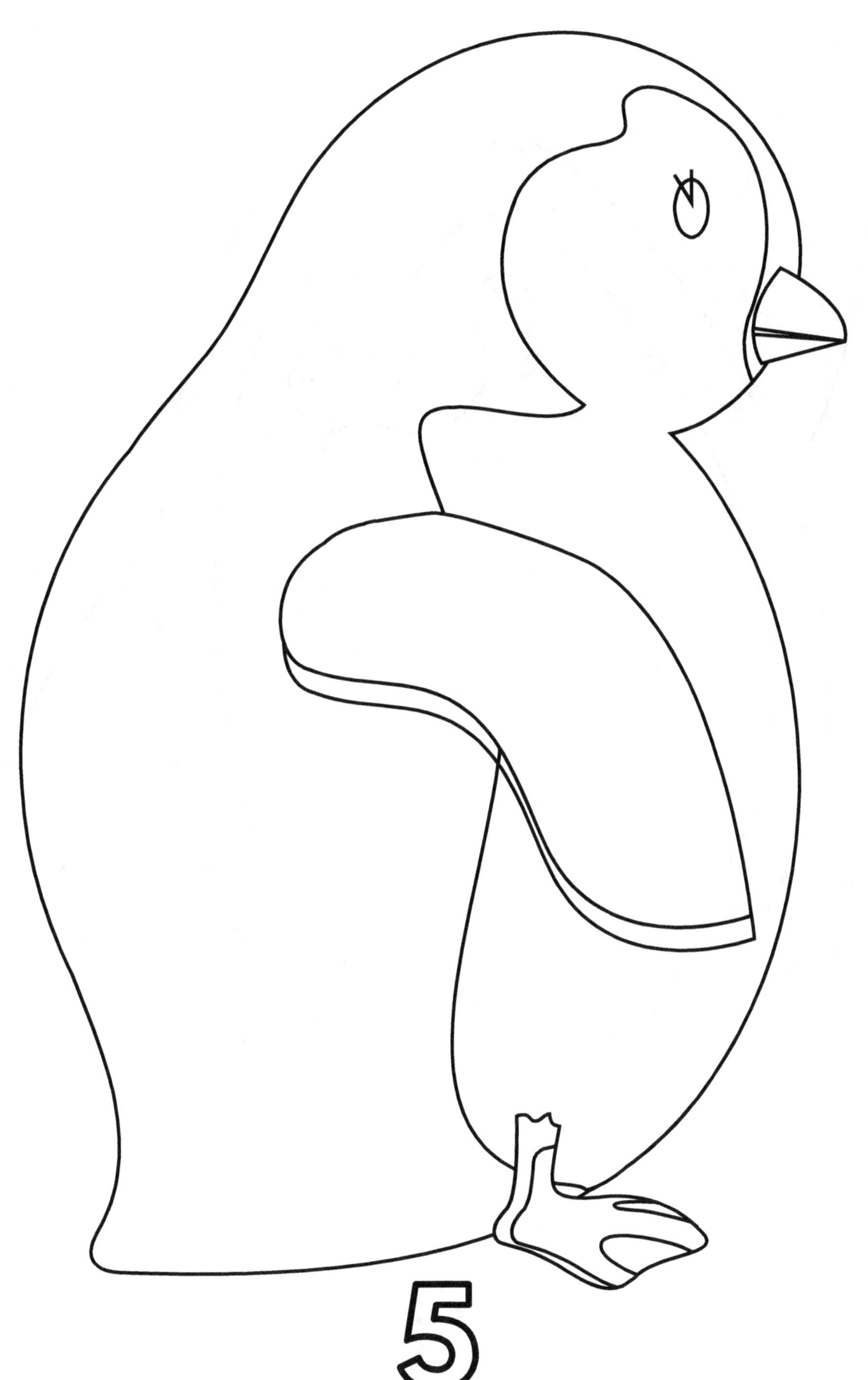

5

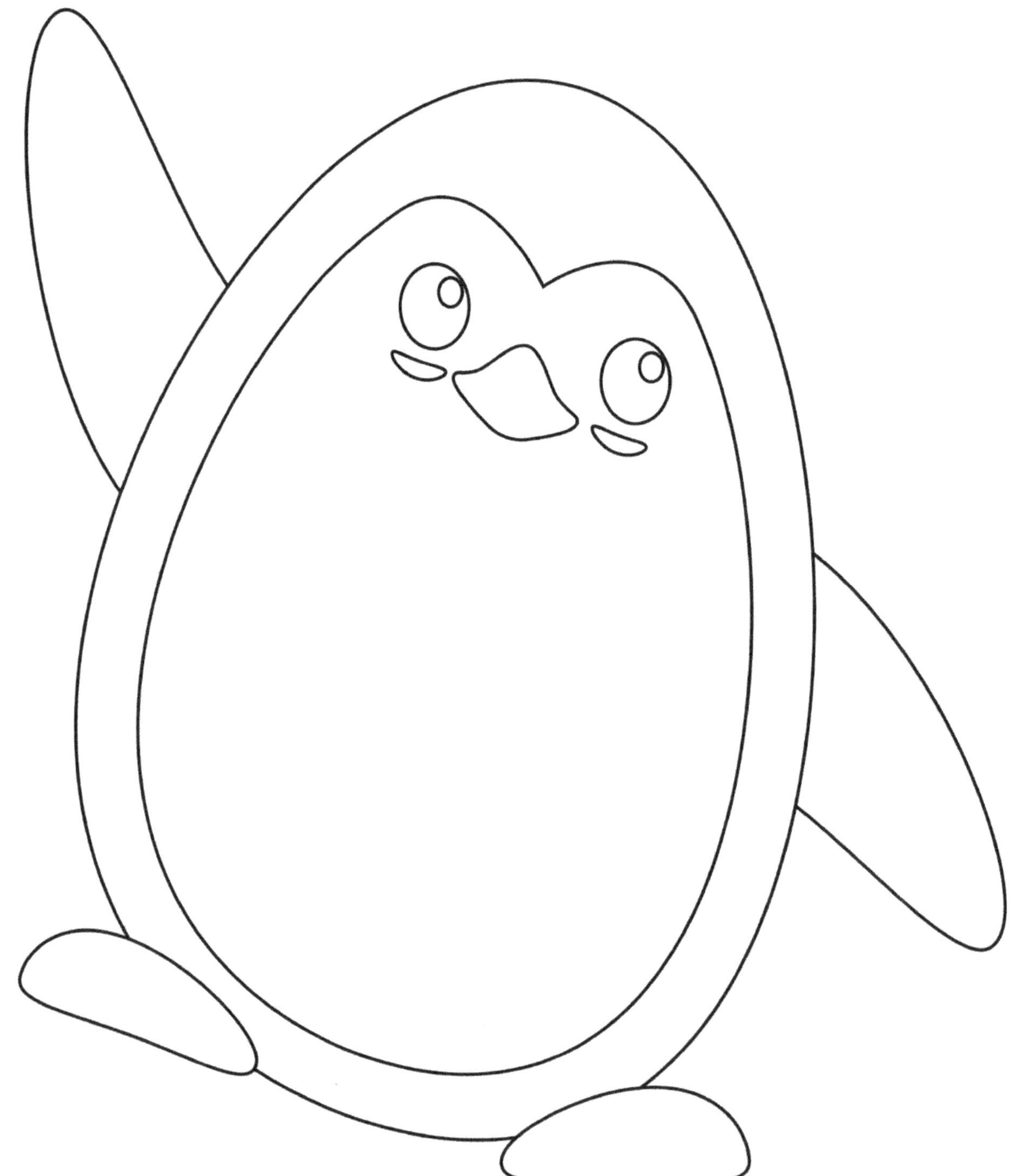

6

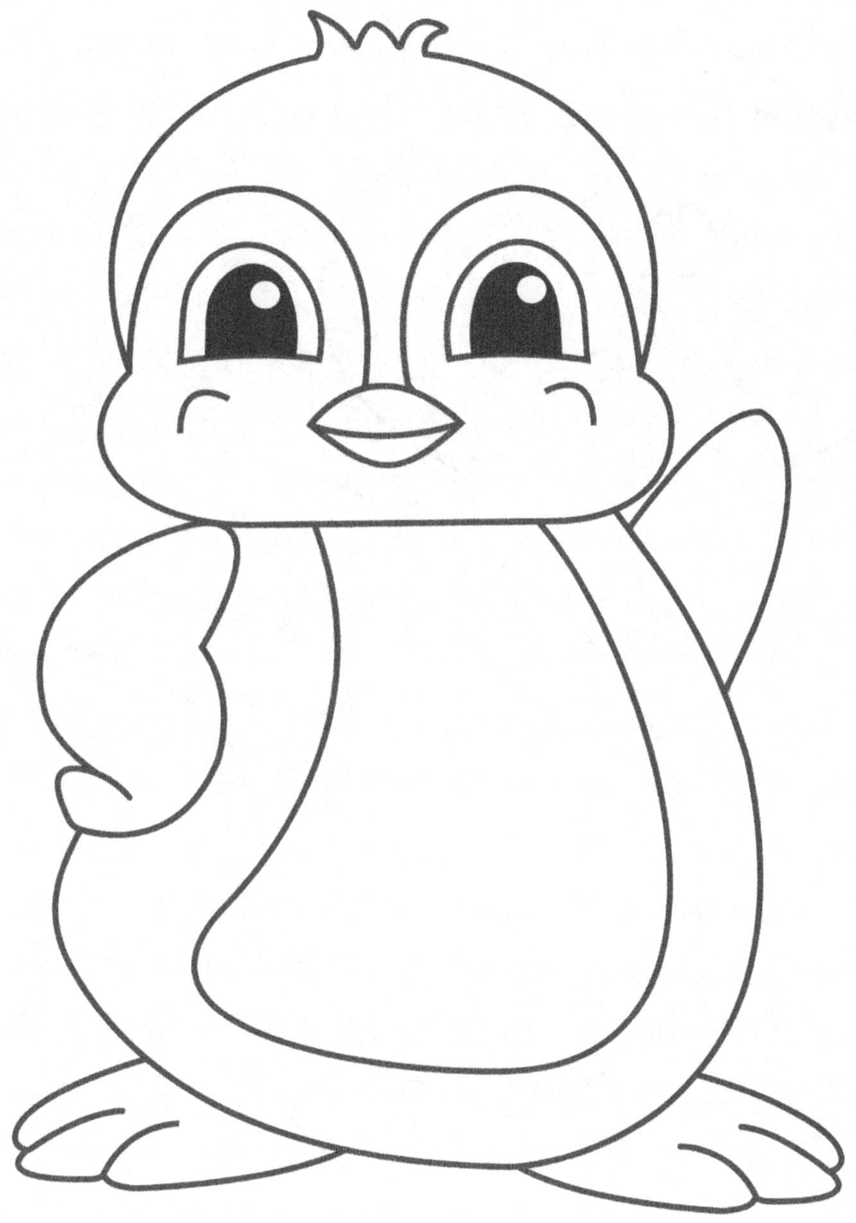

7

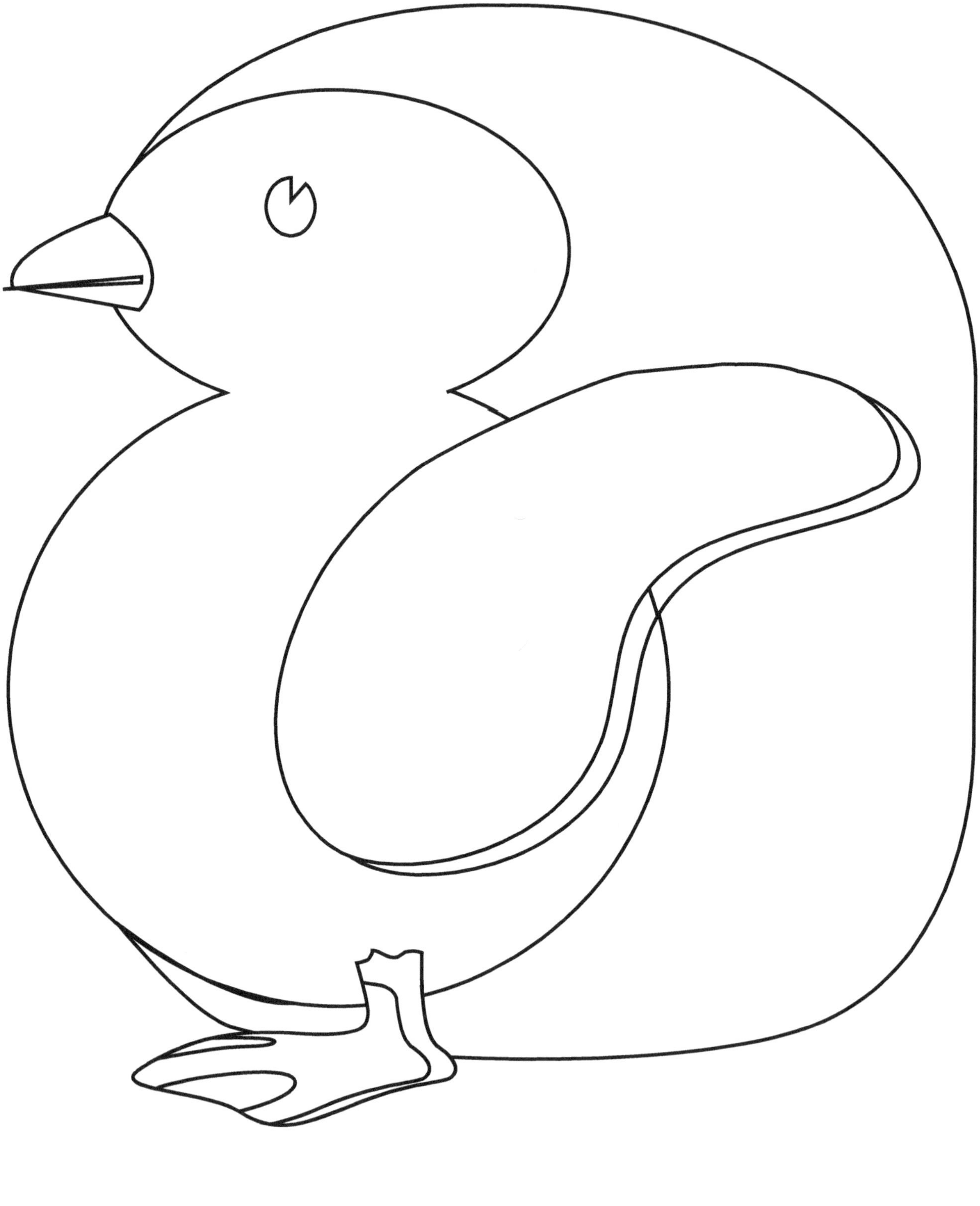

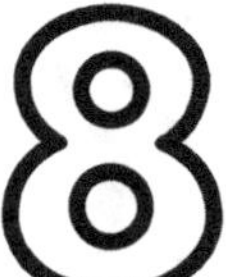

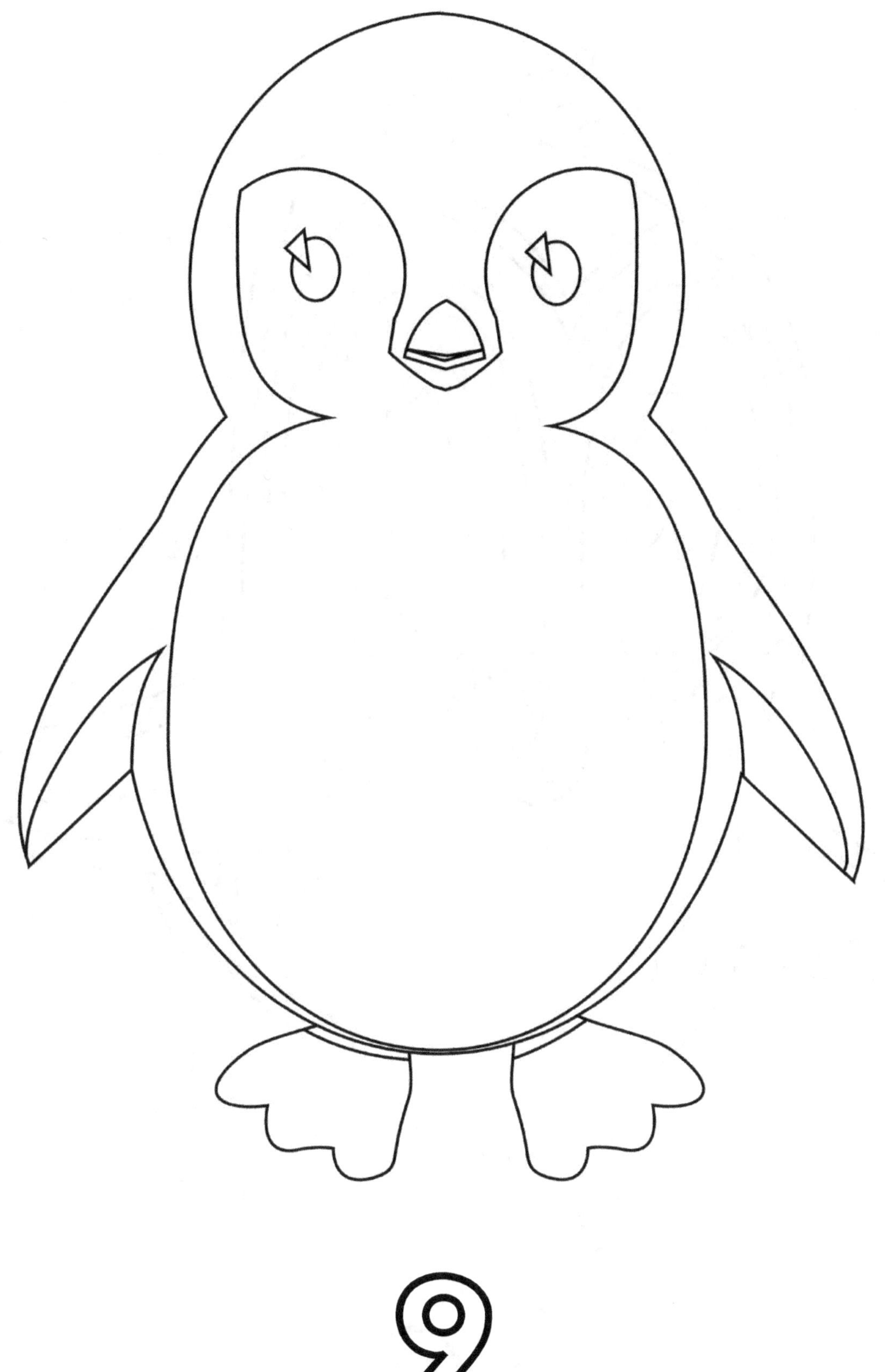

9

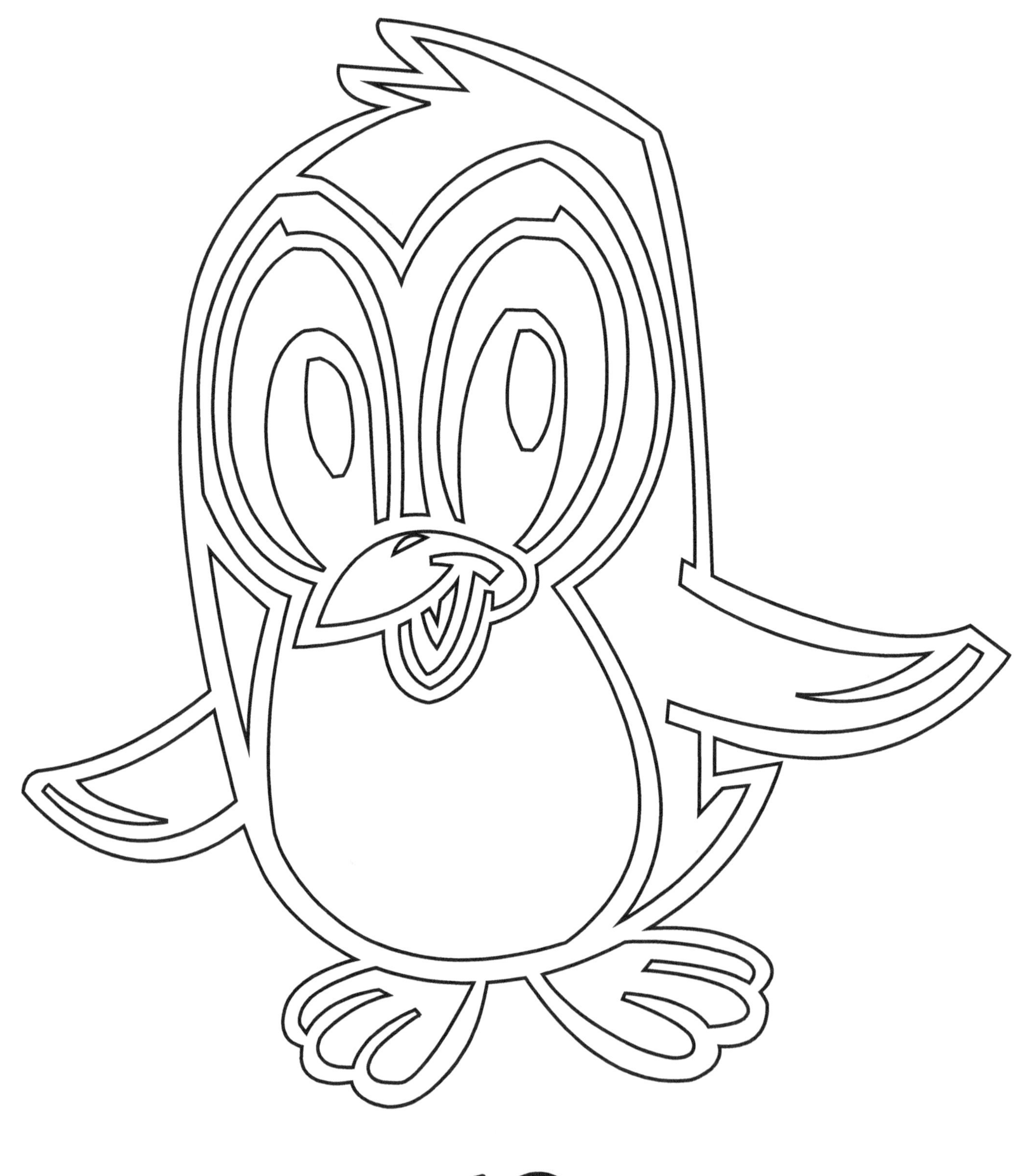

10

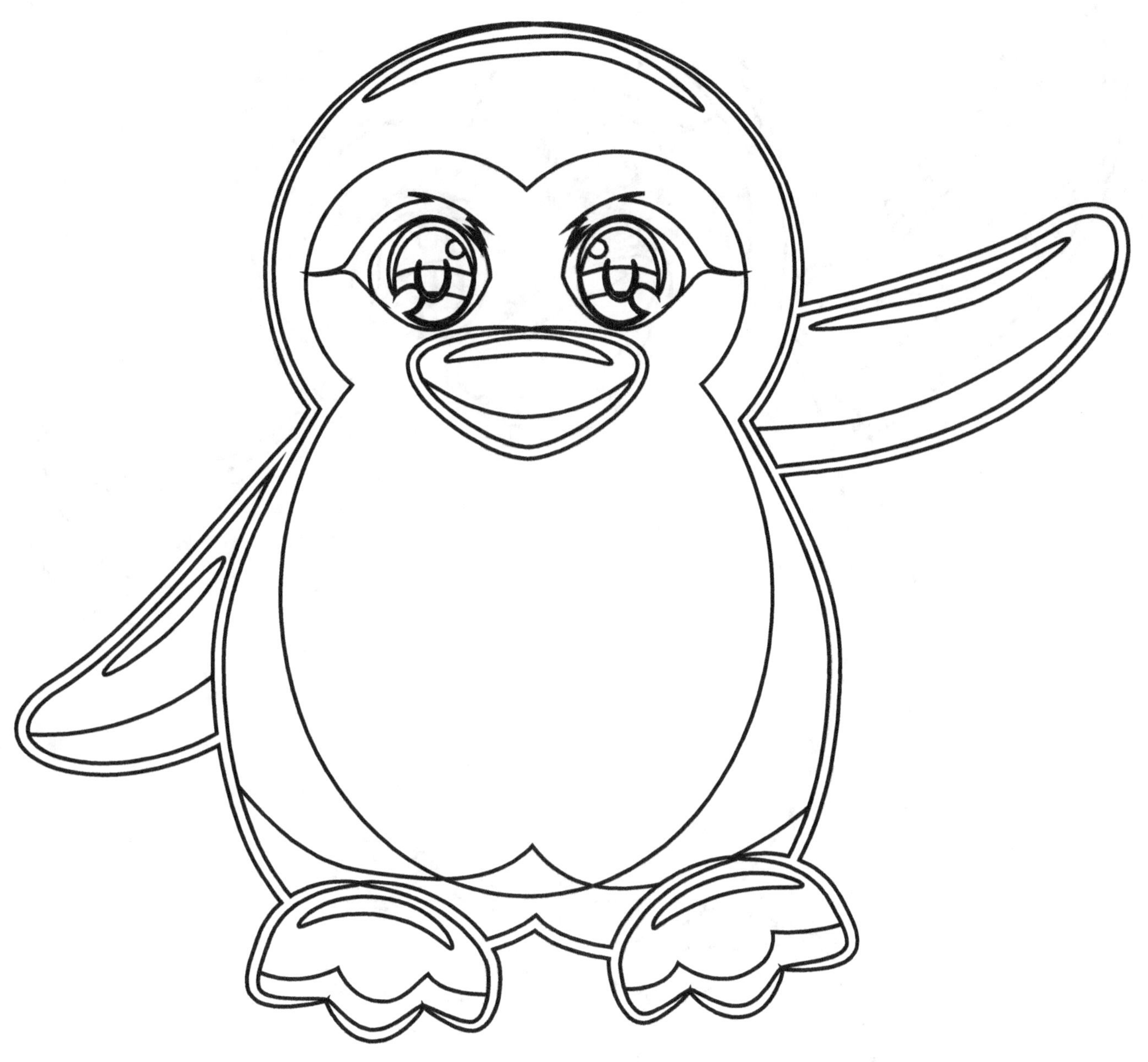

11

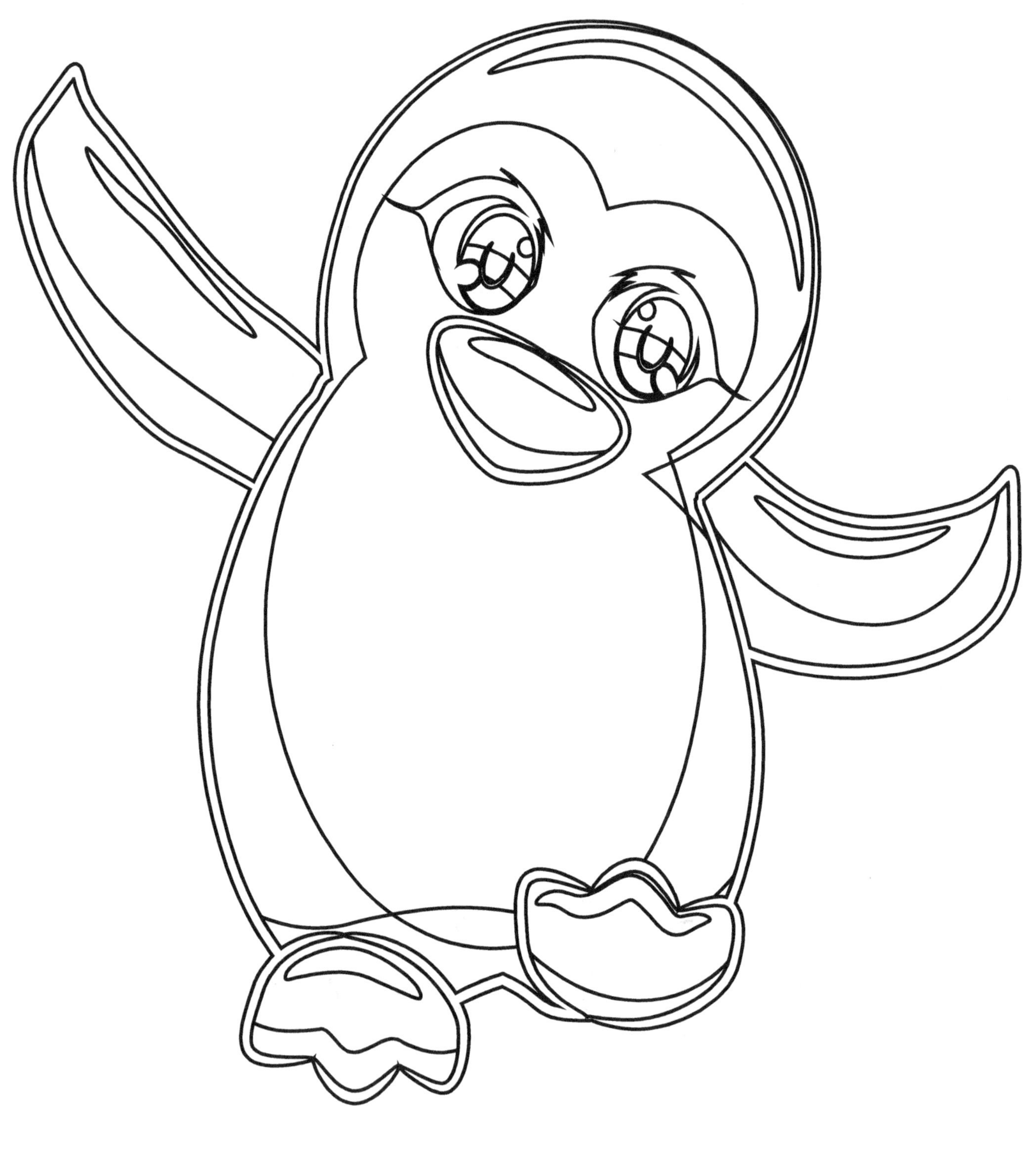

12

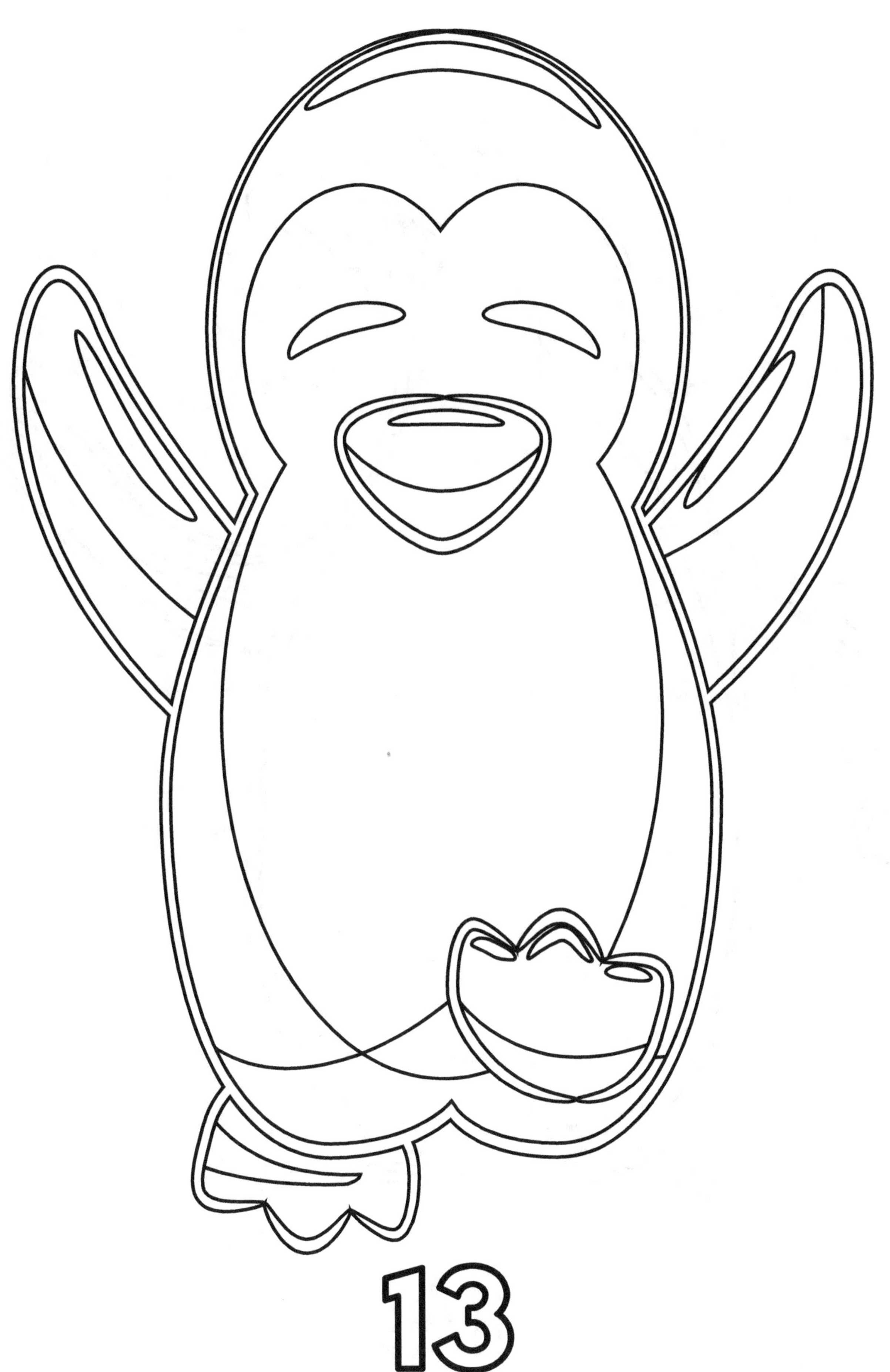

13

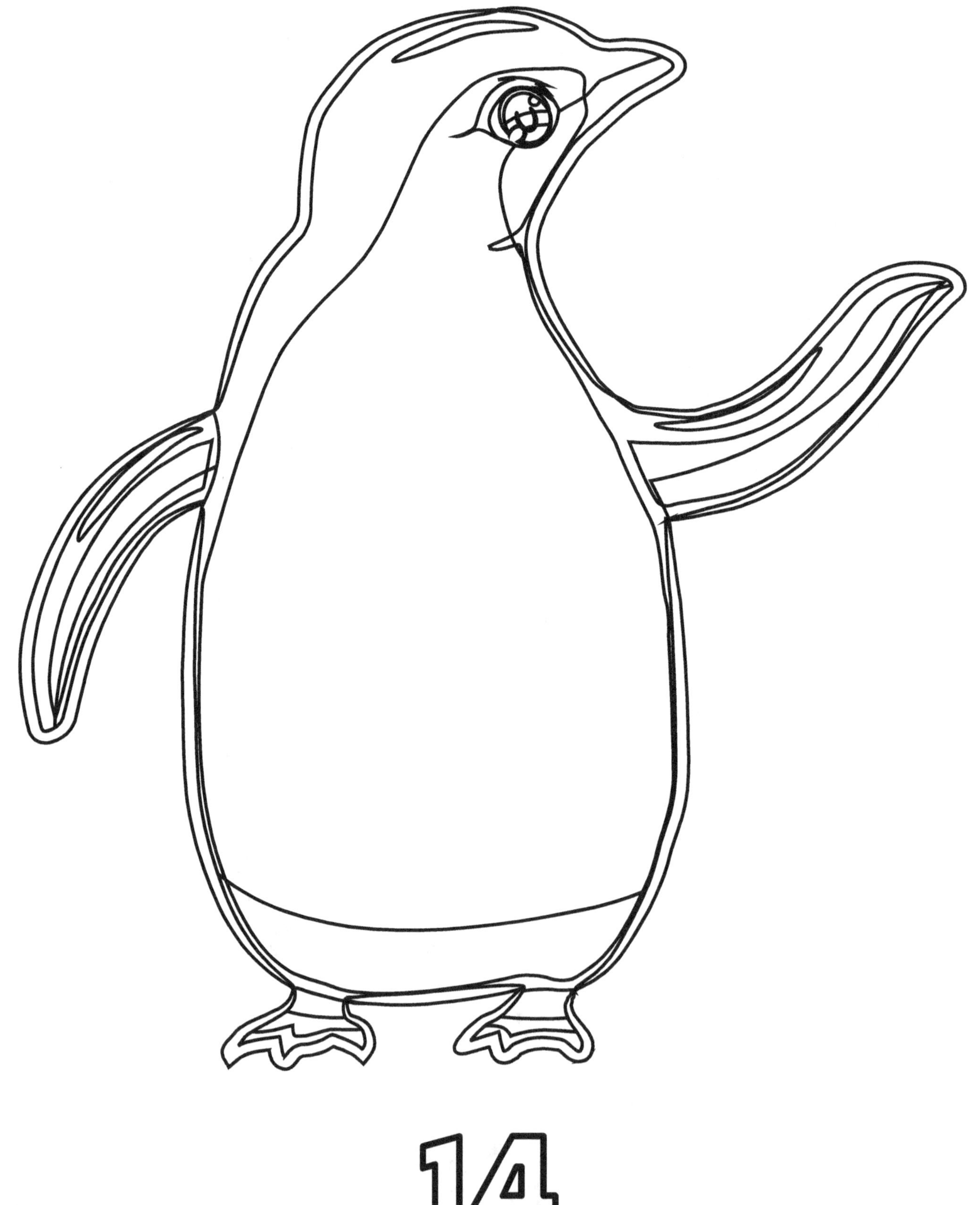

14

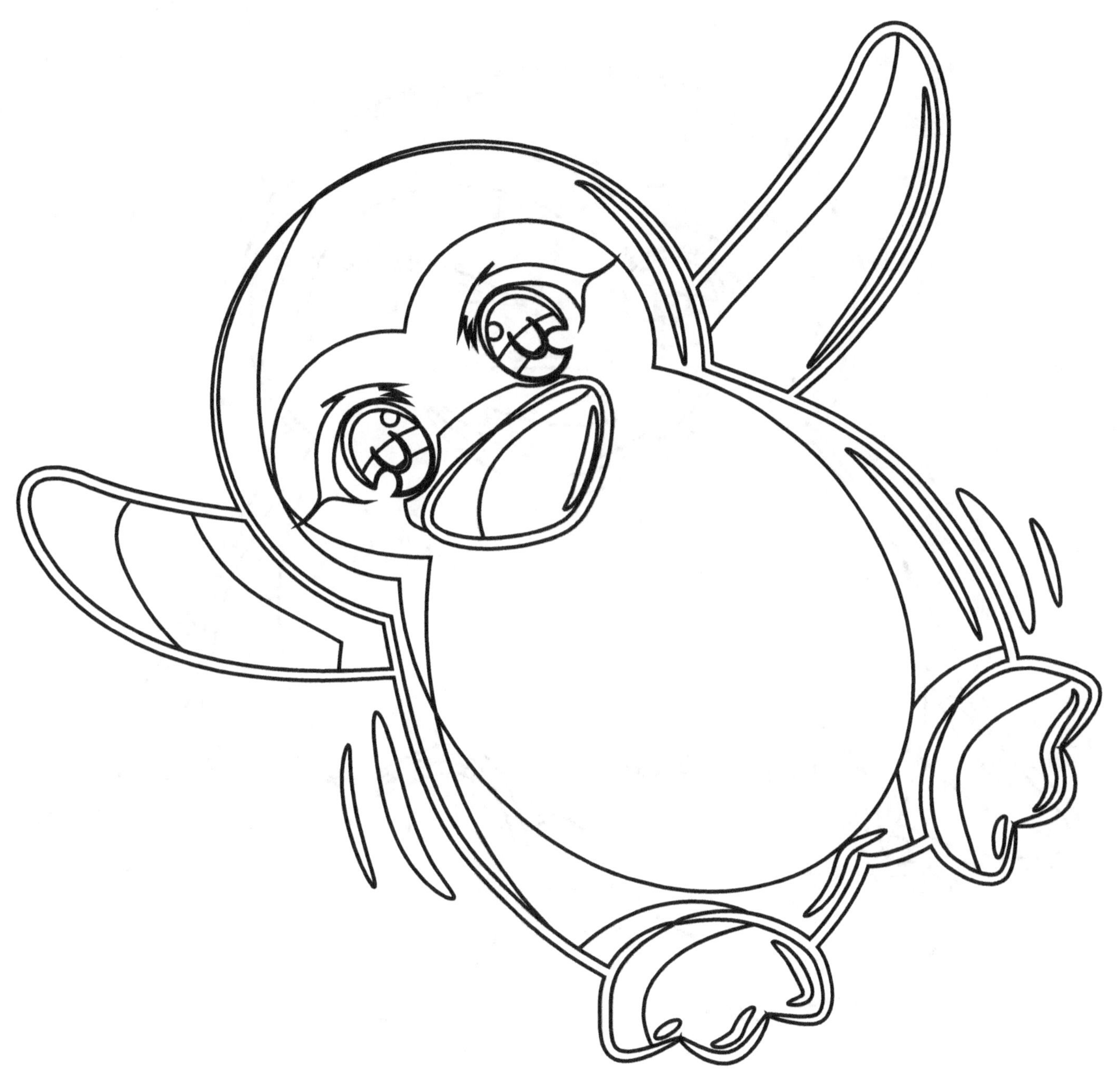

15

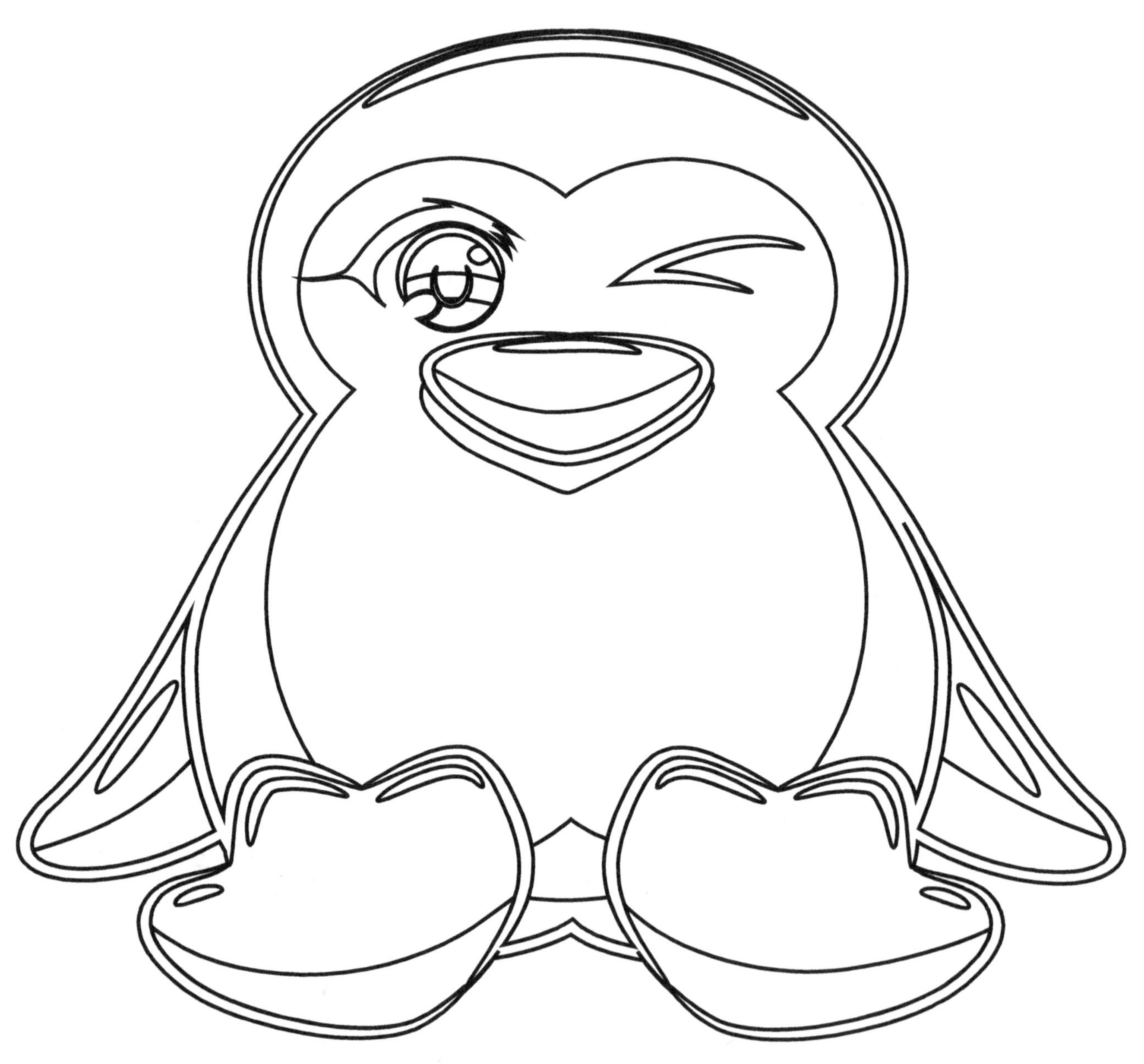

16

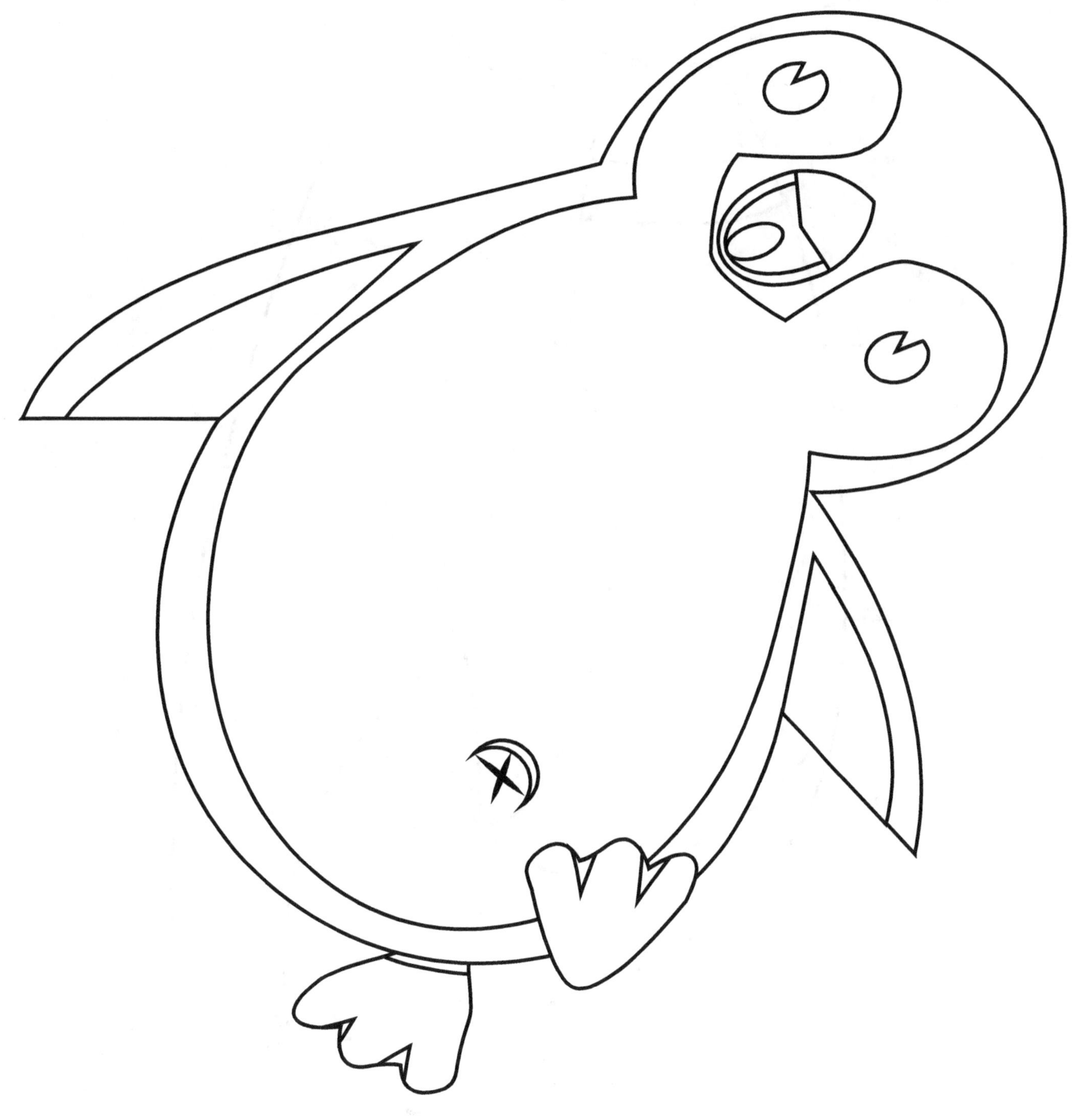

17

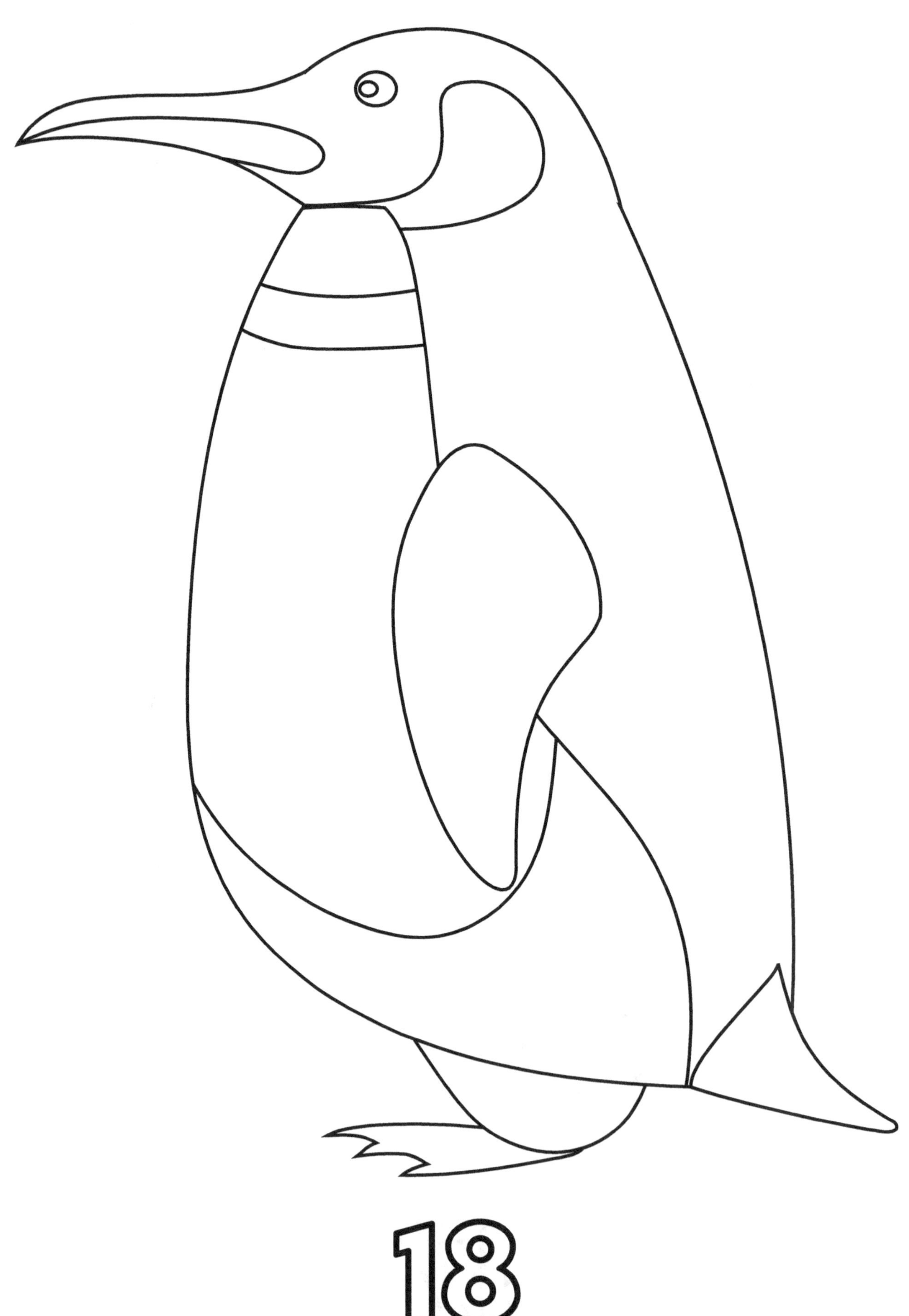

18

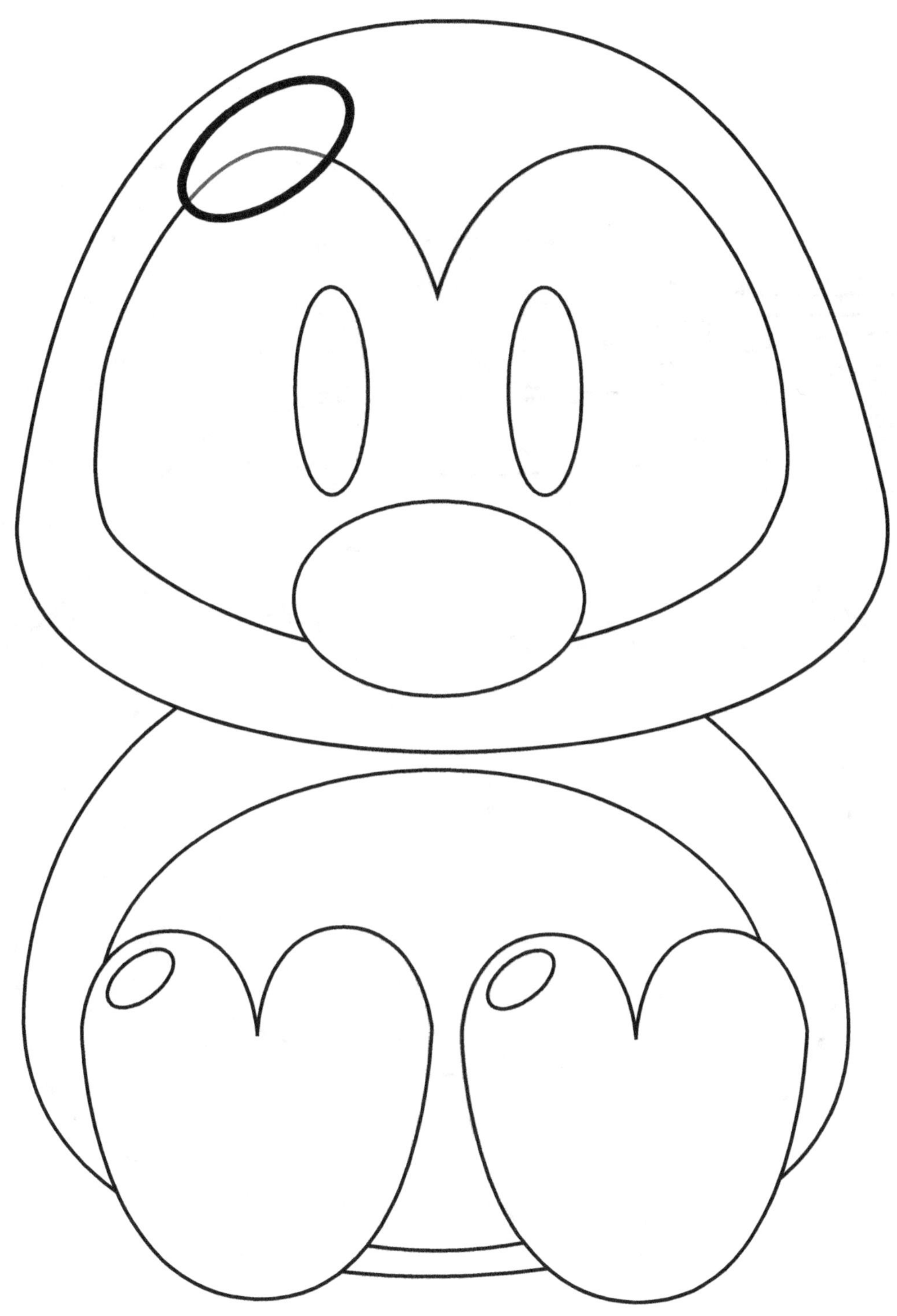

19

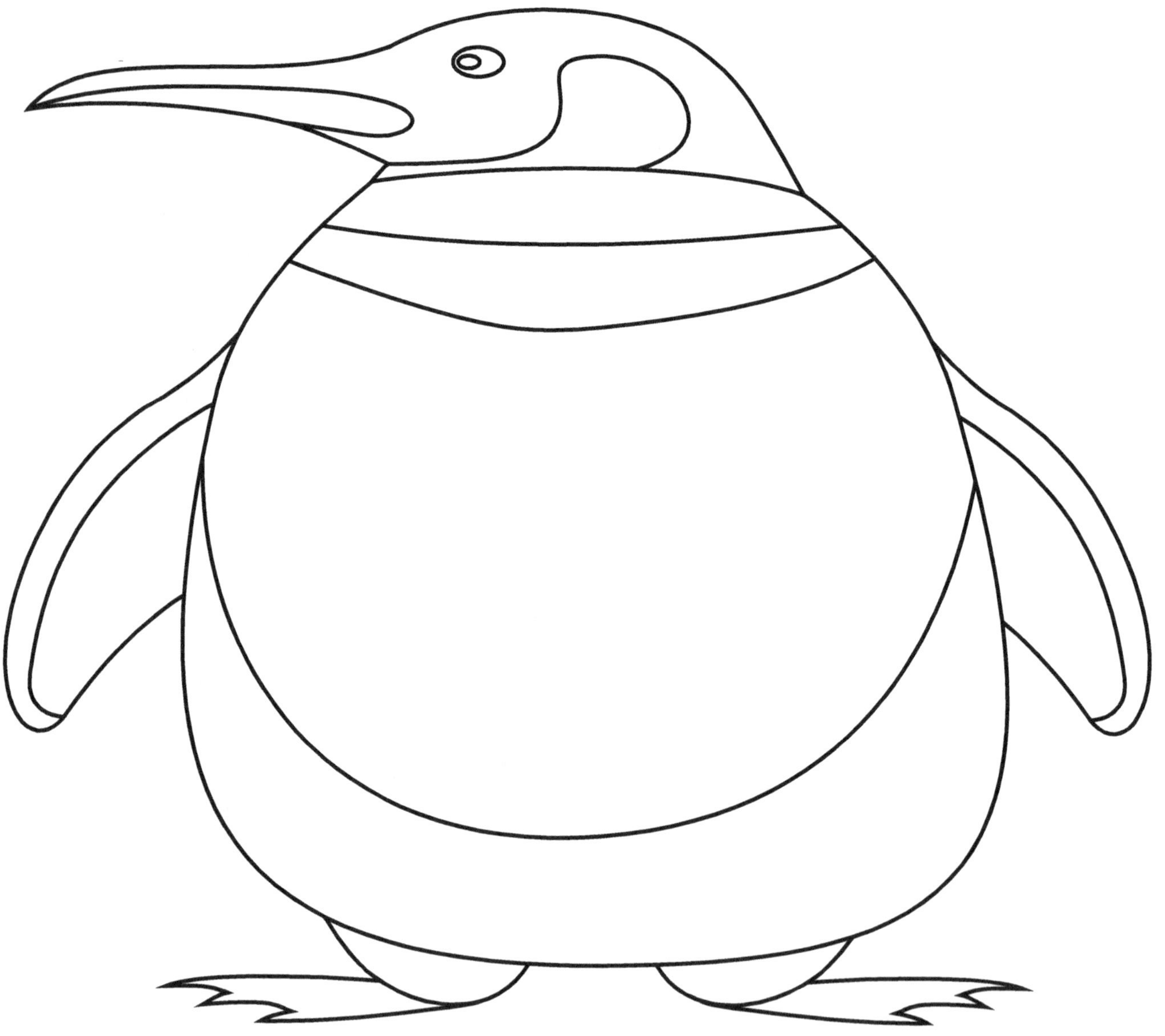

20

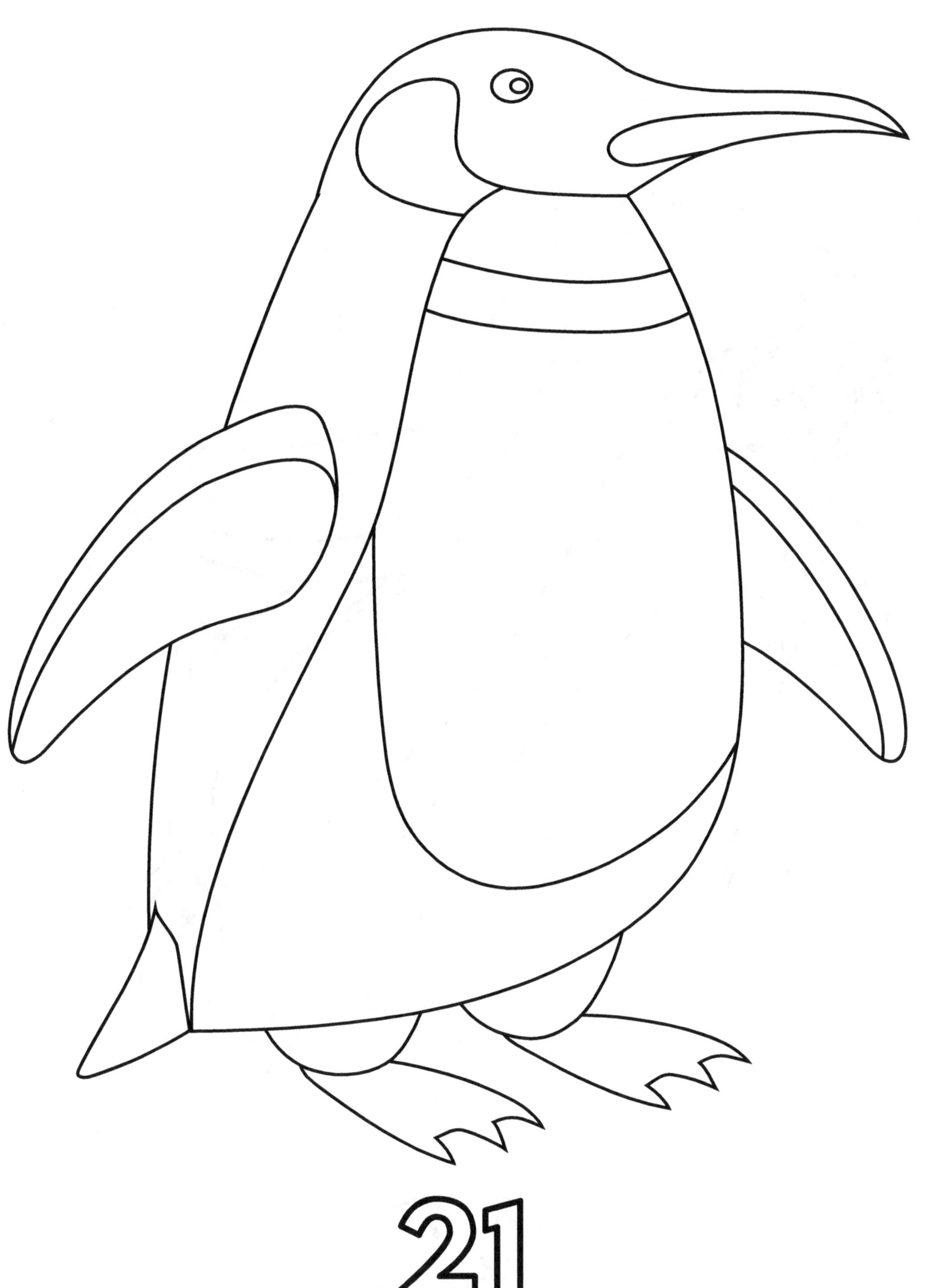

21

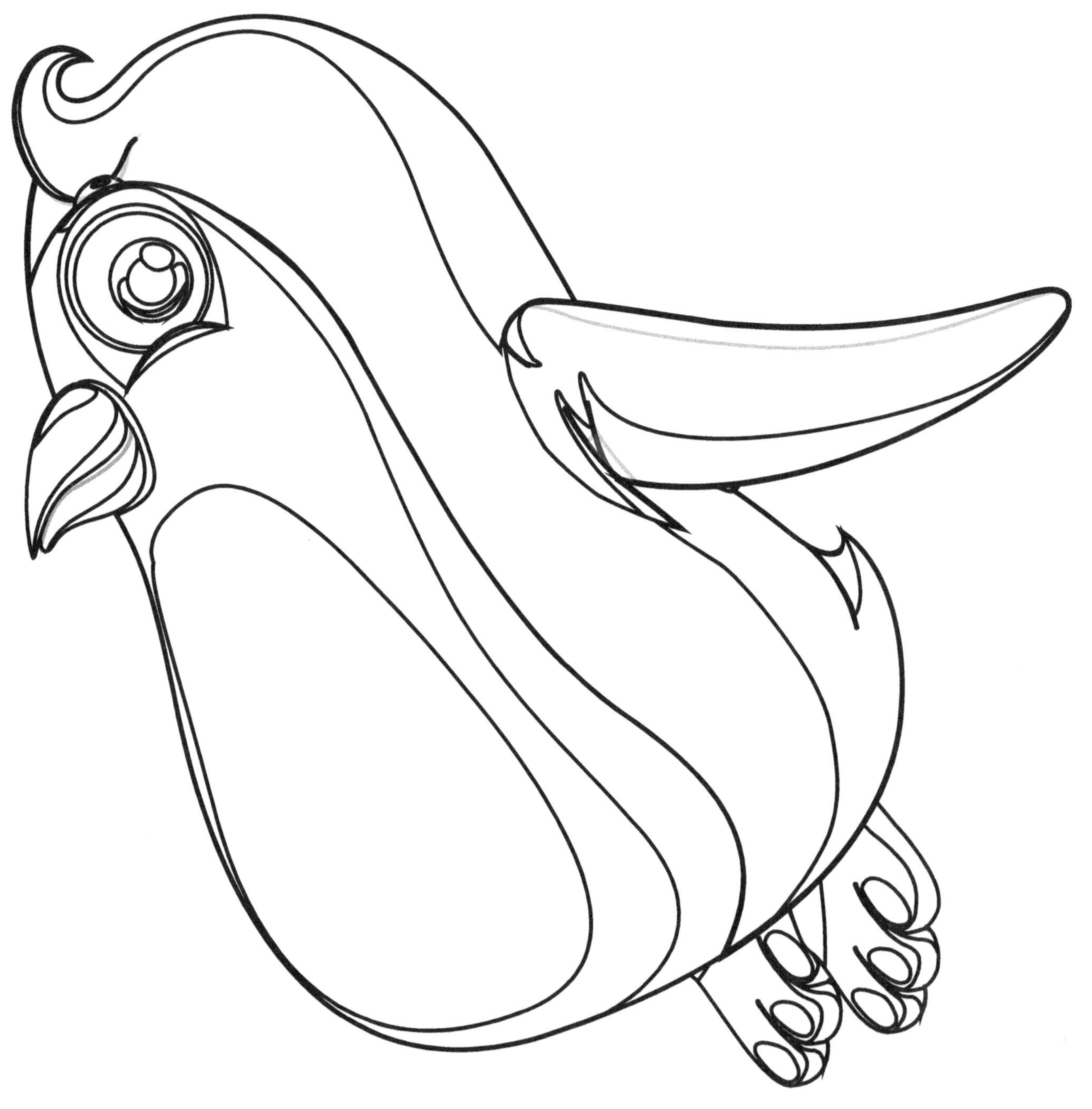

22

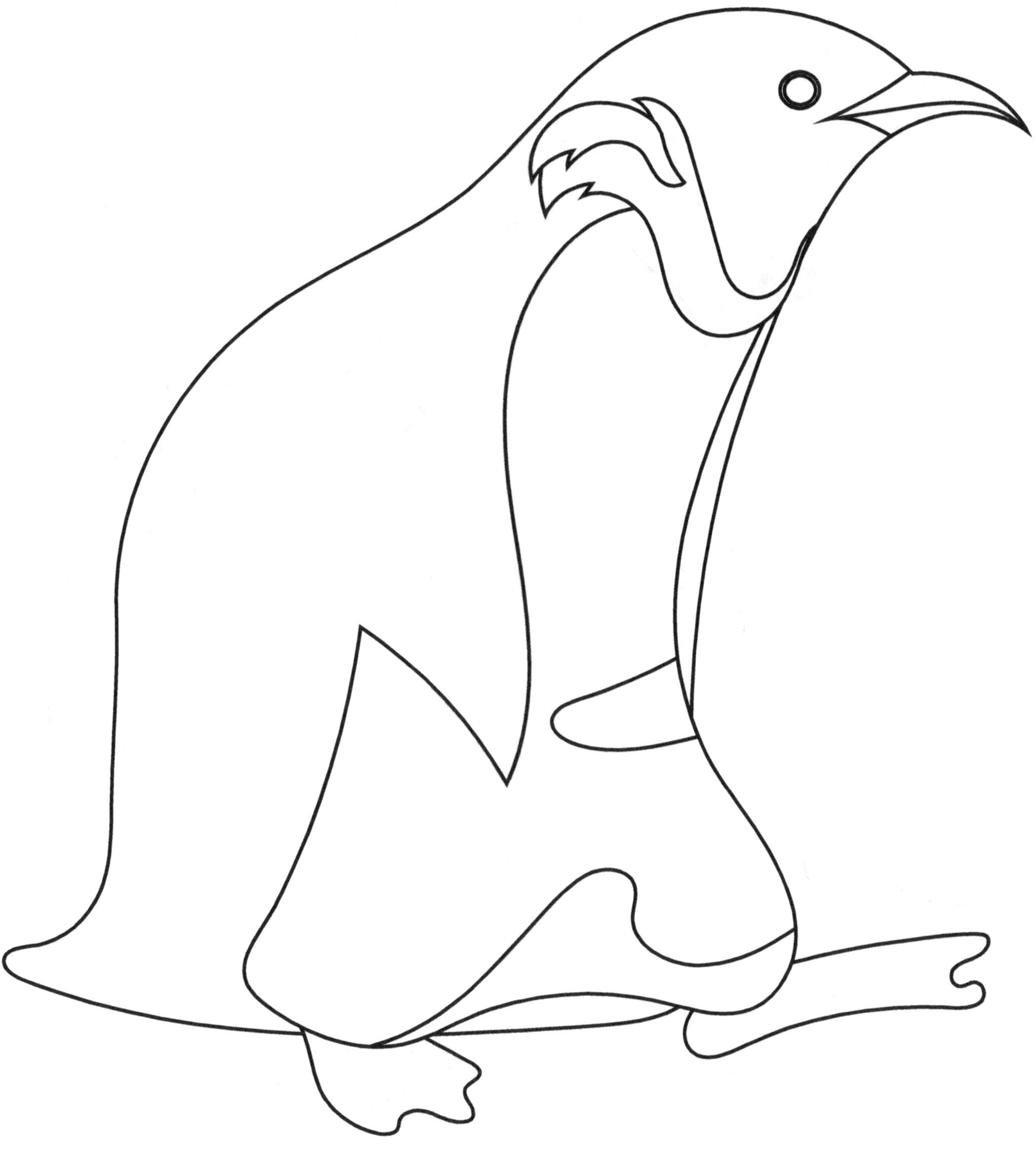

23

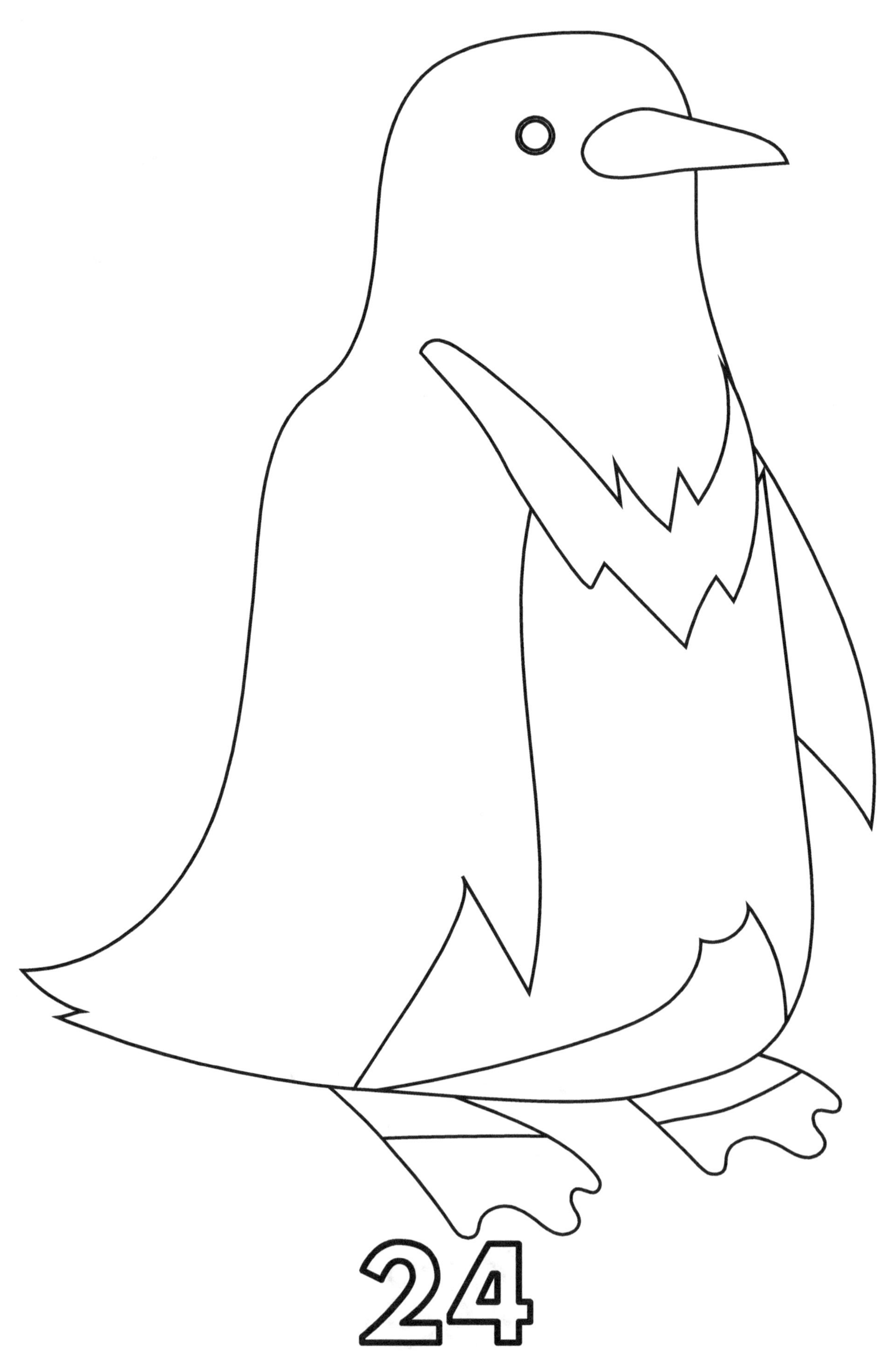

24

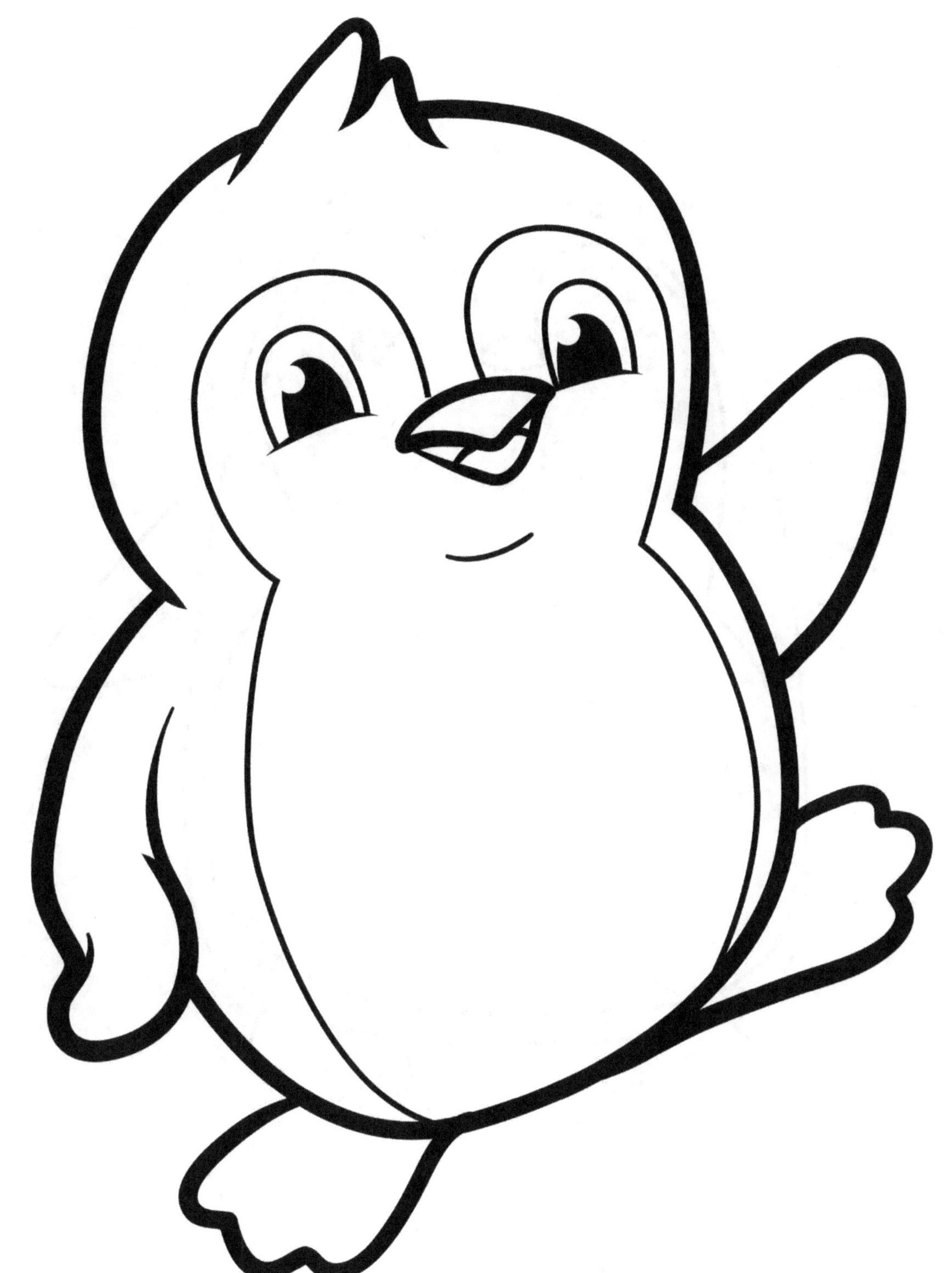

25

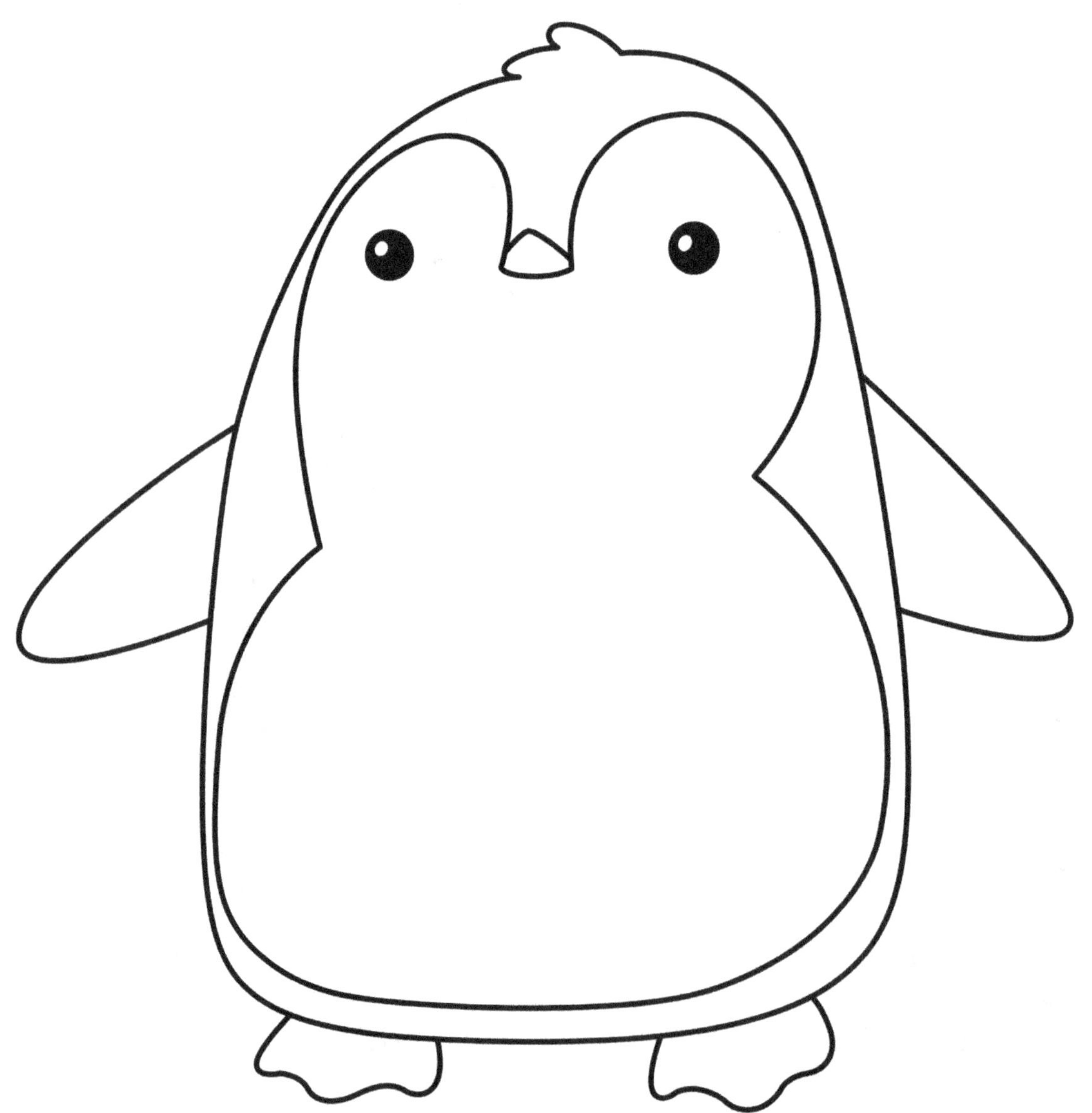

26

TRY TO PAINT PENGUIN

27

28